Effective Leadership:

The Dynamics of Spiritual Authority

Bishop Jerry L. Maynard

Effective Leadership: The Dynamics of Spiritual Authority
By: Dr. Jerry L. Maynard
Published by True Vine Publishing Co.
P. O. Box 22448
Nashville, TN. 37202
www.TrueVinePublishing.org

Cover Design by: Michael Thompson
www.MichaelDavidMedia.com

Table of Contents

Overview 5

Understanding Spiritual Authority 7

Obstacles of Spiritual Authority 12

The Power of Obedience 24

The 3 Ds of Leadership 29

Structure and Coordination 33

Goals, Objectives & Timetables 45

Dynamics of Motivation 62

Overview

When we discuss successful leadership within the church, we must understand that although we are a religious order, we are also an organization. There is an old saying, "Don't be so heavenly-minded that you're no earthly good." As it pertains to the success of the Christian "organization and structure" we must take heed. Many people balk at the idea of organized religion as a negative. They misunderstand the idea of Theocracy. The idea that God will bring all of our desires to pass like a fairy God-parent is errant. We must organize, delegate, and work to bring about God's will. Therefore, anointed leadership is imperative.

Within this workbook we will learn:
- Ø The true purpose of organization within the Church;
- Ø The difference between God-appointed leadership and delegated authority;
- Ø Effective leadership structure and departmentalization;
- Ø Clarification and establishment of a single vision;
- Ø Goal setting, timetables and follow through;
- Ø Cognitive aspects of organization;
- Ø The dynamics of motivation;
- Ø And so much more...

Understanding Spiritual Authority

The first and most important key to effective leadership in the church and as a church leader is understanding Spiritual authority. Just as corporations have a leadership chart which defines the positions and roles of each employee, so the Body of Christ has a chain of command. We must understand who leads and who follows.

The Bible tells us clearly that "Christ is the head of the church." Therefore, there should be no question concerning from where our direction should come. In order to lead effectively, we must understand God's order.

God's authority represents God Himself. Man was created in God's image and given authority through the Holy Spirit. This authority comes with purpose in service of God and His church. Sin against power is more easily forgiven than sin against authority because the latter is sin against God and we must know the authority of God.

We first must accept that our positions as leaders come from God. 1 Cor. 12:28 states, *"And God hath set some in the church, first Apostle, secondarily Prophets, thirdly Teachers, after that miracles, then gifts of healings, helps, governments and diversities of tongues."*

"God has set" the authority of the church. There is no leadership and no authority save what God appoints. No matter how well you speak and how influential you may be, you are not a spiritual leader unless God says so.

Authority is God's choice, not man's attainment. As leaders, we must be secure in this fact. There will be those who challenge our authority. There will be those who seem to be better, more knowledgeable, more skilled, or more charismatic than we.

As leaders, we must learn to utilize the gifts and talents of those who follow us and not be intimidated, threatened, or jealous of these people. With this knowledge of God's appointment, leaders can walk in the confidence of their calling.

The Failure of King Saul

King Saul is an example of one who failed to walk in Spiritual authority, who disobeyed God's absolute word, and was insecure in the authority God gave him. Let's go over a few examples.

Saul Usurps God's Appointed Authority:
In 1 Samuel 13, as Saul waited for the Prophet Samuel to arrive to offer a burnt offering, he decided the prophet was taking too long. Only Samuel was authorized by God to burn offerings before the Lord on behalf of the Israelites. Saul had become so puffed up in the leadership role he had gained that he figured he had the authority to make such a decision. He figured his authority gave him authority over all, so he bypassed the prophet and decided to offer a burnt offering of supplication for himself. To reject God's delegated authority is an affront to God.

Was the concept wrong? No. The Lord did honor burnt offerings and supplication from the people when they prayed unto Him and entreated His grace. However, God has set a chain of command to do so. God does not honor concepts, practices, or well-intentioned actions. God only honors anointed authority and obedience. As the spiritual authority, God does not honor anyone else's authority over the authority that He has given you. Don't be intimidated by those who think they have more education or training than you, because God only honors your position.

Saul Usurps God's authority:
In Chapter 15, when God told Saul to "smite Amalek, and utterly destroy all that they have, and spare them not; but slay both man and woman, infant and sucking, ox and sheep, camel and ass," Saul chose his own rationalization, sparing the king and keeping the valuables as spoil.

Saul failed to understand that spiritual authority is not spiritual *partnership*. As leaders, we don't have an equal vote with God. His authority is supreme. There is no vote, no discussion, and no compromise. Your anointing does not give you a seat at the decision-making table. Even as spiritual leaders, we must submit whole-heartedly to God's absolute rule. No matter how large or small the command, we must follow without question.

Saul wasn't secure in his God-given authority:
Saul spent the remainder of his reign intimidated and threatened by David, a young, harp-playing child. Although Saul had good reason to be threatened (after ruining his legacy through pride and disobedience), he still displays a lack of ultimate submission to God's authority. Saul's

attempt to kill David was another example of his refusal to submit to God; believing instead that he could, somehow, stop God's plan and cancel God's appointment of David. How arrogant can you be? He still had an opportunity to walk in humility and submit to God's will, but instead, he tried to stage a mutiny and kill God's chosen king.

Within these examples, we see many of the challenges we as leaders will face. Whether it be outside challenges to usurp our authority, or internal challenges to reason with God to see things our way; we must understand, trust in, follow, and obey God's order of authority.

Walk *only* in the authority that God has given you. Understand that only God's authority is ultimate. As the apostle, you don't have the authority of the prophet. As the prophet, you don't have the authority of the teacher. As the teacher, you don't have the authority of the apostle or prophet. Instead, we must submit to the representative authority as instructed in the Bible.

*"Let **every** soul be subject unto the higher powers. For there is no power but of God: the powers that be are ordained of God. Whosoever therefore resisteth the power resisteth the ordinance of God"* (Romans 13:1-2).

Think About It!

1. Can you think of a time when someone attempted to usurp your authority? How did you handle it?

   _____
   _____
   _____
   _____
   _____
   _____

2. Has there been a time when you tried to "Partner" with God about an issue? How did that work out for you?

   _____
   _____
   _____
   _____
   _____
   _____

3. How should you respond when intimidated by the talents, skills, abilities, or social appeal of others under your leadership?

   _____
   _____
   _____
   _____

The Obstacles of Spiritual Authority

Within the Body of Christ, we are confronted with tremendous obstacles. None of which are insurmountable; rather all of which are not only mountable, but equally solvable. In order to enhance our posture in our jurisdiction and local churches, we must understand the problems with which we are confronted. Some of the problems can be described as follows:

1. Lack of Communication
2. Lack of Cooperation
3. Lack of Solidarity
4. Lack of Economic Growth and Stability
5. Lack of Membership Growth

Lack of Communication:

Communication is of the highest order as it relates to leadership and spiritual authority. The Bible tells us "faith cometh by hearing." We can't even grow in faith without communication. A leader who has not mastered the art of communication will find his membership scattered and divided.

If there is a communication problem within the church, the problem lies within the leadership. It is not the responsibility of the followers to seek the vision. The sheep don't lead the shepherd to water, the shepherd leads the sheep. If your membership and leaders are not following the vision of the church, then the leader must take an introspective examination of his/her communication. Effective communication can be achieved with the following:

Repetition: It's not enough to tell the body once or every once-in-a-while what the vision is. The vision must be repeated and adopted into the culture of the organization. It must be reiterated in every meeting, reviewed, and updated. The mission should be stated so much that people memorize it verbatim. It is at this point that all actions, energy, and efforts are synchronized.

Written: Habakkuk 2:2 tells us to "write the vision and make it plain upon the tables, that he may run that readeth it." Your church should have a written declaration of your church mission; whether it be a banner or painting on the wall, or even if written in your church's weekly bulletin. There is a reason the Holy Bible is the oldest living document in human history. It is God's mission and vision for Humanity. If writing out the vision is important to God, it must be the same to us.

Bishop Jerry L. Maynard

Think About It!

1. Write out at least 3 creative ways to communicate your churches vision to your members and the community:

   _____

   _____

   _____

2. How effective has your communication to your church and community been? If good, how can you make it better? If bad, what will you do to improve?

   _____

   _____

   _____

   _____

3. Are you taking full responsibility for the promulagation of your ministry's message, or have you relied on others to share it? How can you take full responsibility going forward?

   _____

   _____

   _____

   _____

Lack of Cooperation:

As spiritual leaders, we are called to be long-suffering. We must work with the most difficult of individuals to lead them to salvation. However, when it comes to progress and success of an organization, non-cooperation is a deal breaker. All members of your leadership must be a cooperating participant. If not, then that person should be relieved of duty.

Cooperation does not mean that they have to agree with every idea the leadership has. It does not mean they are not allowed to challenge decisions in a healthy debate for the good of the body. However, once the leader has decided to move forward, after considerable counsel, it is time for the delegated leaders to cooperate and move with the vision.

Non-cooperators cause a plethora of problems within the body including but not limited to:
- Spreading discord
- Sabotaging plans and church efforts
- Changing the course of direction and
- Ultimately destroying and dismantling the organization.

However, cooperating teammates:
- Increase the strength of the team by carrying the weak areas of the team with their strengths
- Expedite the achievement of the mission
- Invite a culture of excitement and teamwork
- Encourage and induce outside assistance

Think About It!

1. Do you have uncooperative Teammates: Yes or No? _____

2. If you have uncooperative teammates, how have they caused division within the organization?

   _____
   _____
   _____
   _____

3. How have your cooperative teammates benefited the organization?

   _____
   _____
   _____
   _____

4. In what ways can you appreciate and encourage further cooperation amongst your team?

   _____
   _____
   _____
   _____

Lack of Solidarity:

Solidarity is Unity. It is not enough to simply be aligned with the Spiritual Authority. The followers must be in solidarity: unified in interests, objectives, standards, and vision. The two can be very familiar but the prudent leader must discern the difference.

Solidarity cannot be manufactured with monetary incentives or forced with threats of losing position. Pastors may often be fooled by yes-men and yes-women who agree with every word the pastor says. Those who never tell you "No" are not necessarily in solidarity with you. To garner the solidarity in your church, it will take fellowship and intimacy.

Leaders must get to know their teams and their teams must get to know the leader. They must bond. This bonding comes from experience. If you're not connecting with your church members on a regular basis, beyond speaking behind the pulpit, how are you bonding with them in order to grow solidarity?

Bishop Jerry L. Maynard

Think About It!

1. What does solidarity mean to you?

_____
_____
_____
_____

2. Think of 6 activities you can start to build intimate relationship and solidarity with your delegated leaders, your church, and your community:

_____
_____
_____
_____
_____
_____

3. How do you recognize the difference between solidarity and alignment?

_____
_____
_____

Lack of Economic Growth and Stability

Money and Ministry is an uncomfortable topic for some ministers. However, you can't have ministry without the finances to do it effectively. Money must buy the food that feeds the poor, pay the electricity which lights the church, fuel the vehicles that pick up those without transportation. When finances shrink, it also impacts the pastor's ability to pursue the vision.

To overcome the economic obstacles within the church, pastors must change their perspectives. Instead of pounding the members to give more, we must focus on the true problems:

Money Management:

This is not to imply that there is mismanagement, but to encourage you to allow an unbiased source to audit your expenses. It is in the nature of man to see what we consider our normal daily expenses as necessary. However, sometimes you may have some expenses that can be reduced or eliminated. Take a second look into your expenses to find areas to trim fat.

Proper Teaching:

Pastors have a responsibility to teach sound financial doctrine about tithing and giving offering. It may be tempting to use our platform to encourage impulsive giving; especially when there is a financial need. However, impulsive giving leaves our members in financial binds, which in-turn affects the church.

I teach my church not to be impressed with charismatic preachers promising extravagant blessing in return for money, but to give as God inspires them. God is not obligated to bless mismanagement. He expects you to listen to Him concerning where to plant your seed and not to toss seed without purpose. By providing sound financial teaching, we maximize the finances of our church.

Financial problems of the body:

Many times, we try to fix the church's financial problems, when we should be fixing the financial problems of the members. The health of the organization is found in the private health of the members. A sick membership equates to a sick organization. A poor membership is a poor church. Our churches will benefit from teaching and training members how to manage their finances and grow wealth, not only through proper giving but proper saving, investing and spending. If pastors taught their members how to grow wealth, the church would be wealthy.

Membership Growth:

When an individual needs more money in his personal finances, he may turn to his current job and request more money, but most likely he won't receive any more than his current salary until his next raise. What he'll usually do is search for a new job. Likewise, pastors can ask for more money from the same members who are currently giving, but most likely you won't get much more than you're currently getting. You need to get more members.

The pressure of financial shortage should not stifle the ministry, but actually cause it to double down on its efforts to bring more people to Christ. The more members you have in your church, the more tithe and offering is provided for ministry.

Think About It!

1. Ask yourself the following question: Have I been a good steward of the funds that have flowed through the church?

2. Does your ministry offer sound doctrine as it relates to tithing and offering?

3. Does your church offer financial management resources to the members?

4. Have financial issues caused you to cut ministry efforts or increase them?

Bishop Jerry L. Maynard

Scarcity of Membership Growth

It is not often that I will share the responsibility of the organizations obstacles with the body. However, when we discuss church membership, we must understand that sheep beget sheep. Shepherds lead sheep but they can't reproduce sheep. This means, that the members must go out and compel more members to join.

However, as leaders, we must serve our members in such a way that they are excited to share their experiences. That is our jobs. We must provide ministry that meets the needs of the members and the surrounding community. Energy attracts energy. Is your church energizing the community by ministering to its spiritual and physical needs?

With the convenience of internet and streaming, what does your church do to draw people away from the computer screens into your church? People go where their needs are met; whether those are social needs, emotional, spiritual, physical, or financial. If we focus on meeting the needs of the community, then the community will meet the needs of the church.

Think About It!

1. Have you taught your sheep how to reproduce? What programs do you have in place that facilitate proselytizing?

   _____
   _____
   _____

2. How are you meeting the needs of your membership and community to encourage growth?

   _____
   _____
   _____
   _____

3. What makes coming to your church more appealing than staying home and watching TBN or watching you via web stream?

   _____
   _____
   _____

The Power of Obedience

Before leadership, comes obedience. No man or woman can lead without being able to follow. The kingdom is God's. He has a purpose to manifest His authority to the world through the church. The greatest demand God has for us is that we obey. 1 Samuel 15:22 "Behold, to obey is better than sacrifice..." For authority to be expressed, there must be subjection. If there is to be subjection, self needs to be excluded and that is done by one living in the spirit. It is the highest expression of God's will.

Have a spirit of obedience:
There is more to obedience than simply doing what you are told. To man, obedience by subjection is acceptable. However, to God, only the spirit of obedience matters. The Bible tells us that "the Lord seeth not as man seeth, for man looketh on the outward appearance, but the Lord looketh on the hearth" (1 Sam 16:7). If you obey with a begrudging spirit, then your obedience is vain. God wants your obedience not out of fear or necessity, but because you love and trust Him.

Having a spirit of obedience does not mean that you aren't a bit uneasy about what God has told you to do. God understands that we live in finite flesh. He understands that our flesh can't see what He sees and can't comprehend the eternal significance of the assignments that He gives us. So He doesn't expect you to be comfortable with obedience but to have a spirit to obey in spite of your discomfort.

The ultimate example of this point is Jesus' proclamation in the Garden of Gethsemane where He asks *"Father, if thou be willing, remove this cup from me: nevertheless not my will, but thine, be done."* Luke 22:42

The Cross was an uncomfortable, terrifying, painful assignment. Jesus' request in this scripture makes it clear that if there was ANY other way to get the job done, Jesus was open to it, but He had a spirit of obedience that committed to obeying God no matter what.

Practice Obedience:
Obedience is a practice. It does not come second nature. It is a practice because we have to grow into it. Because God does not speak audibly to us, we have to learn God's voice and how He gives us direction. Obedience is a practice because sometimes we may get it wrong and we will have to go through the practice again to get it right. It is a practice because sometimes we may think we are being obedient when in fact we are not. God is patient and He knows those who have a pure heart to obey and those who have a rebellious heart.

Practicing obedience to God also means practicing obedience to man. Spiritual authority is of God, therefore when you obey the spiritual authority as unto God, God will bless you as a result. Even if the Spiritual Authority is errant; if you walk in the spirit of obedience—first to God and then to man—then God will honor your obedience. If the spiritual authority is errant and God tells you not to follow, then your first obedience is to God.

Be Subject to the Anointing, not the man:

It is important that we qualify this idea of "obedience to man" because many sects and cults are founded based on this idea that questioning man is questioning God. We must follow man as He follows God and no man can follow God without God's anointing to do so. The Spirit of God anoints, therefore John warns us in 1 John 4:1 *"Beloved, believe not every spirit, but try the spirits whether they are of God: because many false prophets are gone out into the world."*

Obedience does not mean ignorance and lack of discernment. Our relationships with God are personal first and then cooperative. Meaning we don't blindly follow man, but we follow the spiritual authority that God—through our personal relationship—tells us to follow. God will tell you, "my anointing is on him. Follow him." God will also tell you, "I have removed my anointing from him. Go to a place I will show you. "

The Obedient Follow Faith, Not Reason:

The obedient walk by faith, not by sight. As we discussed earlier, the finite human mind cannot fathom the eternal significance God's assignments have. Abram (later Abraham) could not imagine the eternal significance his obedience would have. All he knew was that God was going to bless him with many children. Abraham did not understand that his actions would lead to the salvation of the world through Jesus Christ.

Yet, he had a choice to rationalize whether leaving his comfort and the inheritance he would have received from his father was worth the suffering and sacrifice he would endure. Had he looked at reason, it would not have made logical sense to leave his home. Yet, his faith is now the source of the hope of the world.

When God gives you an assignment or God's spiritual authority gives you an assignment, obey. Know that God does nothing for cheap thrills. All of His commands have eternal significance. Will your obedience be printed on the pages of eternity, or will you be a blip of what NOT to do?

Obedience is higher than works:

Obedience to God is the greatest act you can take. Many times we feel that God or our Spiritual Authority is using us beneath our potential. I remember as a young preacher serving at a church where I was painting the church, sweeping the floors, and taking out the trash. I knew the calling of God on my life. I had been used by God to heal the sick, but there I was sweeping and cleaning.

I could have decided that I was too good for that and sought out to start my own church. But my skills, gifts, abilities, and even anointing would have been meaningless outside of obedience. As a result of my obedience in those days, I am where I am today. God is not like the professional sports leagues who overlook character because of talent. God is not impressed with what you can do, but how you can obey Him. If you can be faithful with a little, then He will make you ruler over much.

Think About It!

1. What does having a "spirit of obedience" mean to you as a leader?

   _____
   _____
   _____

2. Do you believe there is a difference between the obedience required of the leader and the obedience of the follower?

   _____
   _____
   _____
   _____

3. Name a time where you were instructed to work beneath your potential: How did you handle this challenge?

   _____
   _____
   _____

4. Explain how we are to "try the spirit."

   _____
   _____
   _____
   _____

The 3 D's of Leadership

Dedication, Dependability, and Determination

Leaders must be inwardly motivated. Leadership is more than achieving a position of prominence so that others may look up to you. Instead, leadership is about seeking to serve for the betterment of others. The weight of leadership can be heavy and requires more than a fondness for admiration to sustain. I have found that leadership, especially for the church, requires three characteristics:

Dedication:

Dedication means to be set apart for deity or religious purpose; to appropriate or devote. As leaders, we must be set apart from the world. We are held to a high level of responsibility—the care and guidance of God's people. This is not to be taken lightly. God expects us to sanctify our minds, body and spirit for this purpose.

If you hired a chauffeur to drive your children around would you be content with one who shows up to work with the smell of alcohol on his breath, or shows up late and unconcerned with your schedule? Would you expect that your driver have proper training and a stellar driving record? Would you not expect your driver to be committed to the most professional and safe execution of his duties?

If we expect such dedication from those who serve us, why wouldn't we expect God to have the same expectations? God expects His leaders to be set aside for their calling. Not focusing their attention on outside distractions, slighting the church in search of other goals.

Dependability:

Trustworthiness is just as important to God as it is to man. Leaders must be trustworthy. Those who follow you must know beyond a shadow of a doubt that you will keep your word; that you will fulfill any vision you set, and see to the end any assignment you set. They must believe that you would not ask them to do anything you wouldn't do yourself. No one can fully trust and follow a leader who doesn't display these characteristics.

God as well will test your trustworthiness. The New International version say is like this: "Whoever can be trusted with very little can also be trusted with much" Luke 16:10. God tests and builds our dependability by starting us off slowly and allowing us to prove our trustworthiness. If you can't show up on church on time once a week, you can't be trusted to be accountable to God's people seven days a week. If you can't share $5, God can't trust you with $1 million. Leaders must prove their dependability to God and man before they can be effective in their call.

Determination:

Determination is defined as *"To be resolute and firm in purpose."* Leading God's people is a challenging job. You will be challenged both physically and spiritually. When you lead God's people, you are on the devil's radar. His goal is to discourage you and tempt you to give up. When Jesus announced his purpose, the first thing he faced was the temptation of Satan to give up His assignment.

Jesus, however, showed us what determination looks like. Though fatigued and at the point of starvation after 40 days and nights of fasting, Jesus rejected food. Though offered earthly rule, celebrity and esteem, He rejected Satan's offer to rule the earth. Though taunted with the idea that He really wasn't who He claimed to be, He rejected Satan's challenge to prove Himself by jumping off a cliff.

There will be many temptations and many challenges that will make you wish you had not chosen to be a leader. However, you must be determined to walk out your call until the end. You must be determined to stay committed through any circumstances, until death, with or without praise from others.

Bishop Jerry L. Maynard

Think About It!

1. In what ways can you show God that you are dedicated to His assignment?

   _____
   _____
   _____
   _____

2. How important is dependability to you as a leader and why?

   _____
   _____
   _____
   _____

3. What is the driving force behind your determination for ministry?

   _____
   _____
   _____
   _____

Structure and Coordination

The structure of any organization begins when people combine efforts for a given purpose. This combination of efforts is called "Coordination". Coordination is the orderly arrangement of group effort to provide unity of action in the pursuit of a common purpose. Coordination contains all the principles of organization; it likewise expresses all the purposes of organization.

These purposes relate to its internal structure. To avoid confusion, we must keep in mind there are always two objectives of organization: the internal and the external. The external may be anything. It consists of the multitude of interests calling the group together, but the internal objective is always the same: coordination.

In any organization, the external objective is not continuous, but in every form of organization, the internal objective must be constant. This internal objective is "organized efficiency," and everything that is essential to such efficiency is expressed in the single word *"coordination"*. Coordination is a constant necessity in organization, essential to the existence of the organization itself. As coordination is the all-inclusive principle of organization, it must have its own principle and foundation in authority, or the supreme coordinating power.

Think About It!

Name 5 External Objectives of your church:

1. _____
2. _____
3. _____
4. _____
5. _____

Are these objectives congruent or diverse? _____

Name the 5 Ministries /Departments required to achieve the objectives

1. _____
2. _____
3. _____
4. _____
5. _____

Most likely, these 5 ministries / departments have diverse goals and missions. However, how can these ministries coordinate their efforts to achieve the overall vision of the church?

_____
_____
_____
_____

Cognitive Aspects of Organization

The Vision of the Church is set by God. The Leader must have a specific mission for the Vision. People need a purpose, a reason to do more. Church goers will support the mission if it is clear and defined. It is the leader's responsibility to ensure all projects mirror the mission of the Church. Leadership must decide what percentage of the church will be involved, how financially vested it will be and what teams will be responsible to see it through.

We are the Body of Christ. From the pastor and elders, to the children and non-members in the community, everyone has a place in the body. The leaders of the church must have a cognitive structure. God, above all else, is first. Working from the top, the pastor and elders of the church are the spiritual leaders. Other leaders would include deacons and servers. It is up to the leaders and the needs of the church as to what ministries will be included in the structure. There are faith ministries that build relationships with God and the church. There are work ministries the build relationships with the church and the community. Every ministry has a leader.

The Foundation of Coordination is Authority

Authority, in this context, is intended to imply theocracy and not democracy. God is supreme power and He delegates to the pastor, (the spiritual leader) who in return delegates to his team of leaders. As we find in Ephesians 4:11, God "gave some, apostles; and some, prophets, and some, evangelists; and some, pastors and teachers." The pastors are appointed by

God, but the pastors delegate authority to ministers in the areas of responsibility, receiving reports from those who work from within their ministries.

Leadership must presuppose the organization. There can be no leader without someone to lead. Leadership requires exercise of a derived authority. We should never confuse power with leadership. **Power-**in the psychic sense - *the ability to do things* – that is distinctly an individual possession.

Think about it!

1. List your key organizational leaders. Do they submit to God's authority and yours?
2. As God's appointed authority, have you sought God concerning who you have delegated over His ministry?
3. As a leader, do you foster and encourage coordination?
4. If attitude reflects leadership, how do your delegated leaders make you feel about your leadership?

The Rights of Authority

When we speak of the power of an organization, we mean this power has become collective through coordinated effort. Authority, on the other hand is a right; a license, an entitlement. Hence, we use the expression **"moral authority"** and may say of great teachers, as was said of Jesus, the greatest of all teachers: He spoke "as one having authority," which means he had a moral right to speak as He did.

In organization, authority is, likewise, a right because it inheres legitimately in the structure of the organization. Rights cannot be divorced from duties. Ineffective leaders seek the rights of leadership but, resist and relegate their duties to others. If authority does not use its rights with due solicitude relative to those duties, it is sooner or later bound to fall. No organization has prospect of stability or longevity without moral factors as its basis.

Think About it!

1. What rights do you have as a leader?
   _____
   _____
   _____

2. What responsibilities do you have as a leader?
   _____
   _____
   _____

3. Do your rights as a leader supersede your duties, or do your duties supersede your rights?
   _____
   _____
   _____

Establishing Departments

The major purpose of organization is coordination. The highest degree of coordination takes place with the department set up. The greatest lack of coordination and danger of friction occurs between the departments and the points where they overlap. When all of your organizational leaders set up a definitive purpose, then Chief Executive Officers can focus on coordination. They can guide the team to ensure major purposes are not in conflict, and the various processes are consistent with the church's agenda to touch the community or reach areas of the city in appropriate, rational, and effective ways. The service rendered must fit the needs of the people.

Departments help divide the work of the church among organizational subunits, allowing you to break up the workload into smaller, more specialized focuses. What would happen if you were building a house and everyone was hammering away at the same nail? The house would never be built, many people would be injured from the swinging hammers and there would be mass chaos. Instead, you have to let the construction workers hammer the nails, the painters paint, the plumbers work on the pipes and electricians work on the electricity. Before you know it, the house is built.

As previously stated, your departments must fit the needs of the people. Don't create departments just to give people something to do. You wouldn't hire a car mechanic for your house construction team. There's no need for him or her. Likewise, take careful consideration to the departments that are developing in your ministry. Remember that every department draws time, energy and resources from the collective body. If that energy is not producing beneficial gains toward the single vision, then it is an unproductive limb. Jesus showed us what to do with trees that don't produce fruit.

Effective Leadership: The Dynamics of Spiritual Authority

Think About it!

1. Who are the specialized workers /Departments in your ministry?

_____

_____

_____

_____

2. Are your departments working toward the overall goal of building your house, or are they working on a different blueprint? How will you ensure all departments have the same blueprint?

_____

_____

_____

_____

_____

3. Match the departments of your church with the following community needs: (If you don't have a department for the need, create one)

Community Need	Your existing Church Department
Homeless	_____
Hungry	_____
Educational Needs	_____
Sick and Shut-in	_____
Imprisoned	_____
Poor and Needy	_____
Childcare	_____

A Single Vision

Keeping with the construction metaphor; there can only be one blueprint by which builders work. Although different workers may be constructing different aspects of the home which require completely different tools, instructions, and even time requirements; they are all adding the necessary additions to a single vision and plan.

There is but one Vision in your church. That is the vision that God has given the Pastor. That God-given Vision must become a part of each member within the church. In a church in which all the major auxiliaries follow one vision and philosophy, the department coordinator must furnish the inter-departmental coordination. The church must be highly developed with uniform standards and methods, particularly in projects, finances and participants.

The inter-departmental coordination streamlines to an even greater degree the amount of effort, energy, and resource required to meet the church's goals. By creating effective and prudent missions and submissions, the organization fast tracks its path to success with greater efficiency. However, it is important the departmental mission does not become a platform for egos, posturing and positioning within the organization. It is a weed of which vigilant leaders must be aware.

One of the biggest challenges in delegating leadership to different department heads is that the church begins to accumulate a bunch of new "pastors". Individuals who believe they have a separate calling from God beyond the "delegated authority" that the Pastor has assigned. There should be no doubt within an organization who the anointed and appointed leader is, and what that leader's vision is.

All mission statements and departmental vision should *UNIFY* with the single vision. It is not enough for your department to have an "aligning" vision. An aligning vision is in cooperation, but it is NOT unified.

For example: if your Vision is to feed 1 million hungry people. Your department's vision should be to feed 1 million people. If your department's vision is to "provide 100 pounds of rice for hungry people," the vision "cooperates" with the church's vision but it is not unified. Once the department has met it's 100 pounds of rice, it stops working. However, 100 pounds of rice only feeds 800 people; far from helping achieve the vision.

Be sure that each department vision is "unified" in purpose. Though objectives may differ, they should all provide one final product. In the church, there are no simple final measures for successful operation of subsidiaries like the profit and lost margin statements in business. Leadership must be intimate and complete, not distant and limited. There must be warm bodies touching at all times. Leaders communicate purpose by reminding the team of the Vision. The team shares that Vision with the people through the structure of the organization put in place by the coordination of the leadership team.

Think About it!

1. What is the vision God has given you?

_____
_____
_____
_____

2. Have you thoroughly communicated the vision to your department heads? If not, what steps can you take to do so?

_____
_____
_____
_____

3. Are you aware of any weeds of ego and positioning in your ministry? _____ (yes or no)

4. Have your department heads provided written Mission statements? _____ (yes or no)

5. Do those statements align or Unify with the Single Vision? _____ (yes or no)

Goals, Objectives & Timetables

A Church with no goals and objectives is just a social club. Goals provide the purpose of any being or organization. Goals define you and goals lead you. Goal-setting within an organization provide the following benefits:

1. Goals propel you forward.

Even an erroneous goal is more beneficial than no goal because they move you forward. Forward motion is progress. Even if you have to change direction, it is far better than stagnancy. Goals act as a GPS; giving you clarity of where you are in relation to where you want to be. Without goals, churches can get caught up in the meandering roads of "church work" and lose sight of "kingdom work."

2. Goals transform mountains into stair steps.

The calling of God is the greatest calling there is. It is grander in scale than the human brain can fathom. Goals and objectives help you to focus on the most important step, instead of becoming overwhelmed with the overall mission. Two famous old sayings state, "The way to eat an elephant is one bite at a time," and "The journey of a thousand miles begins with the first step." The goals are to eat the elephant and walk a thousand miles. The objectives are the first bite and step.

3. Goals hold us accountable:

Without goals it becomes easy to wander away from our plans. Goals hold us accountable to the actions we take. If the goal is to feed the hungry, we can easily recognize that hosting a clothing drive is antithetical. Even though a clothing drive is an admirable and Kingdom-focused activity, it is not leading you to *your* goal.

Think About It!

1. Have you written out the goals of your church and the goals for each department? Take time to write out the 5 most important goals for your ministry:

   _____
   _____
   _____
   _____
   _____

2. Are your goals practical for your ministry?

3. Have you had to or do you need to make changes to your goals?

4. Do you promote goal-setting not only within your church but in the personal lives of your team?

Goals Have Boundaries:

As the leader, you must be careful not to try lead every goal. When Moses tried to judge all the concerns of the people, his father-in-law Jethro told him:

"Thou wilt surely wear away, both thou, and this people that is with thee: for this thing is too heavy for thee; thou art not able to perform it thyself alone" (Exodus 18:18).

Even Jesus had specific goals. When the Canaanite woman requested Jesus' help to deliver her daughter from a demonic spirit (Mark 7:24-30) Jesus' response was "I am not sent but unto the lost sheep of the house of Israel." Here we have a powerful example of goal-oriented specificity.

Jesus understood that in His flesh, He could not do for everyone what He was capable of doing. As church leaders, we must stay faithful to the post God has assigned to us. If you leave your post, even for benevolent, well-intentioned reasons, you compromise the integrity of God's vision.

Think About It!

1. Have you tried to be all things to all men? Describe the burden that has placed on you.

   _____
   _____
   _____

2. What are the boundaries God has given you and your goals?

   _____
   _____
   _____
   _____
   _____

3. How do you maintain your boundaries; and if you have not, how do you plan to start maintaining your boundaries?

   _____
   _____
   _____

Our Goals must represent God's vision:

Before setting any goals, we must understand our place in the chain of command. As church leaders, we are faced with the challenge of galvanizing a community of diverse personalities to see one goal and coordinate their efforts toward that goal. Therefore, our goals must represent God's vision for the local church. There is no room for ego or personal ambition. Before we set any goals, we are to seek God as instructed in Proverbs 3:6 *"In all thy ways acknowledge Him, and He shall direct thy paths."*

Man's goals are short-sighted and can only reach what our eyes can see and minds can conceive. But Isaiah said, *"men have not heard , nor perceived by the ear, neither hath the eye seen, O God, beside thee, what he hath prepared for him that waiteth for him."* (Isaiah 64:4) How can we lead anyone into an eternal destiny?

If Moses would have plotted the escape route, he would have led them around the Red Sea, not through it. If they took the rational route, the Egyptians would have overtaken the Israelites and taken them back to slavery. Instead, God had to break the will and spirit of Pharaoh with the miraculous water crossing so that Pharaoh would never again try to enslave God's people. Know that you are limited in scope and yield your goals to God.

Think About It!

1. Have you adopted God's vision for your organization, or are you asking God to adopt yours?

2. Describe a time when your plans were short-sighted and limited in scope, but God's outcome worked out for your good:

_____
_____
_____
_____
_____
_____
_____
_____
_____
_____
_____

SMART Goals:

It's not enough to know goals are important, but practical implementation is required. Some may think that goal setting is fundamental, but there are many people who have not been properly trained to set goals: specify what they want, measure their progress, take action, set realistic expectations, and time their goals. In this section we will discuss SMART Goal Setting for Church leaders. SMART Goals is a well-known acronym to help people break down the goal setting process. S.M.A.R.T being

S- Specific
M- Measurable
A- Action-oriented
R- Realistic
T- Time-oriented

What are Goals? Quite simply, goals are what you want to be, do, or have. It's that simple. Every person sets daily goals. When you wake up and decide what you want for breakfast, what time you want to get to work, what time you want to leave work. Goals are set daily. Everyone wants something greater than they currently have. So it's not enough to simply say you want to spread the Gospel around the world, or you want to feed 1 million people. You must break the goal up properly so that you can attain it.

Specificity is Essential:

God is a specific God. Thus our goals must be specific. Generalization yield little if anything. Focus on the specific goal God has given you and don't entertain distractions. This does not mean that you don't have other goals. It means that all of your goals lead to the one specific goal. Each goal must be a supporting beam of the primary one.

There is a concept called "intentional congruence". Intentional congruence is coordinating your efforts to feed into each other to achieve a specific goal. An example of intentional congruence can be seen in the following diagram of how diverse efforts all feed into one goal:

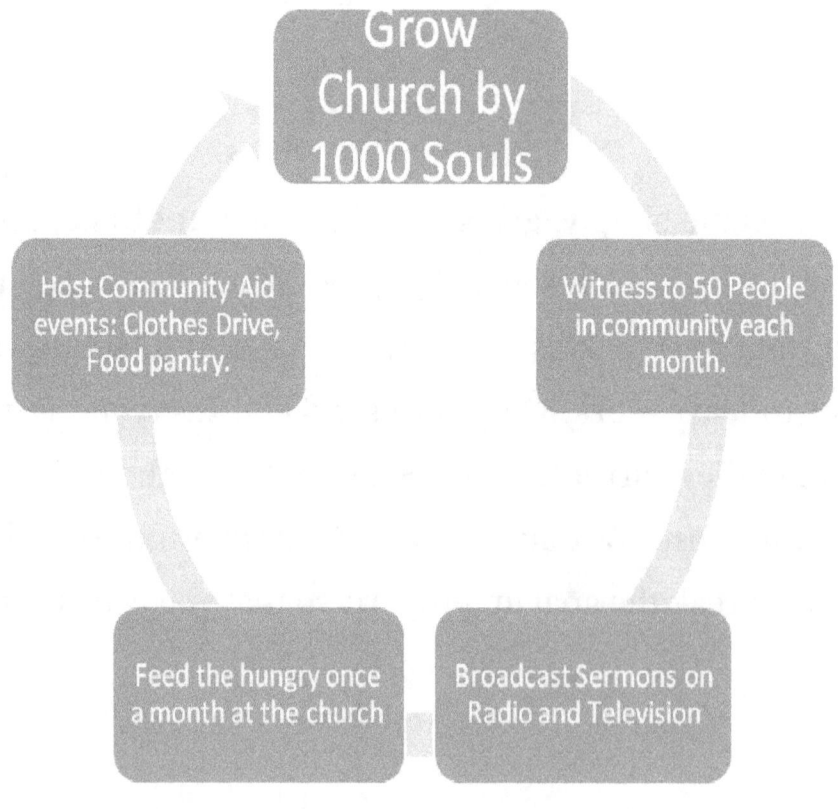

Effective Leadership: The Dynamics of Spiritual Authority

Think About It!

Think about your current primary goal. How have you, or will you, create intentional congruence?

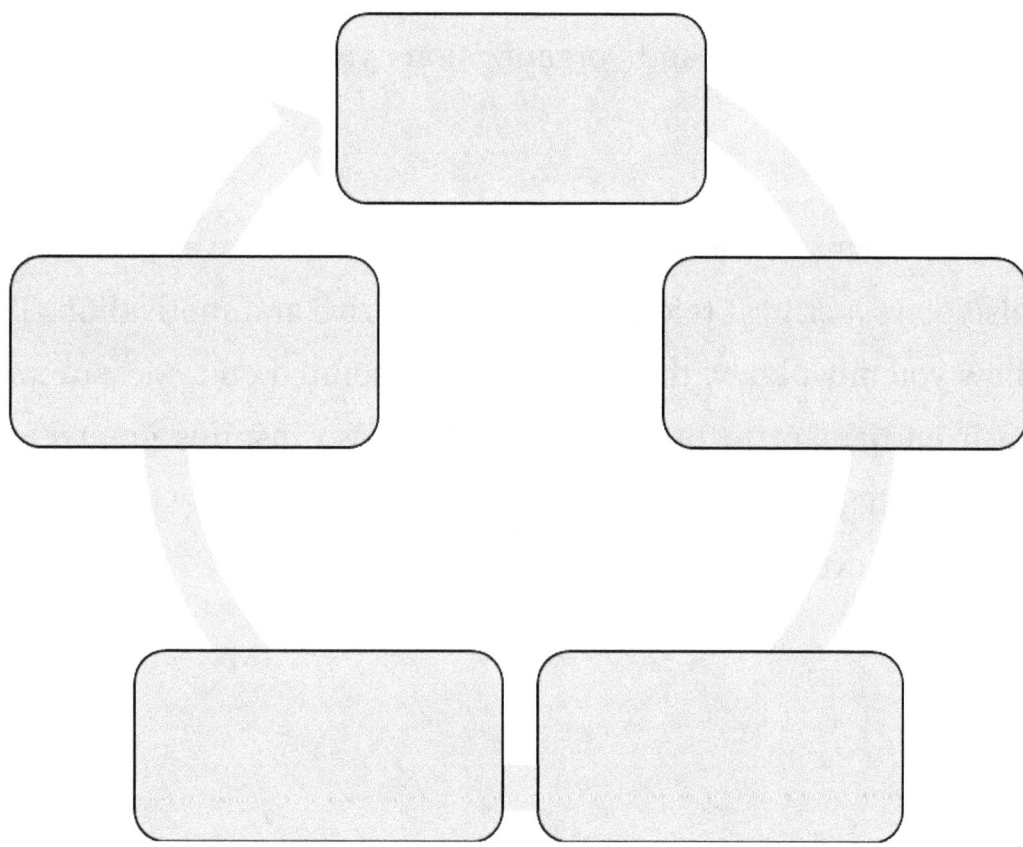

Measure Your Goals:

Can Goals be measured? Absolutely they can, and if your goal can't be measured then it is destined to fail. Every goal can be broken down into quantifiable metrics. Whether you are raising money, building membership, increasing devotional time, or increasing quality time with your family, you should be able to break that goal down into calculated blocks of time and effort. These measurement also help you to inventory the time, resources, people, money, and organizations you have and will need to meet your goal.

By measuring your goals and objectives, you gain clarity on your progress which also plays a critical role in maintaining drive and motivation. Those who follow you must know that there is an appointed end. Measurements allow each participant to project the end. It also inspires greater effort when they see that any additional resources, time, or energy they offer will expedite the achievement of the goal.

Think About It!

Take time to Measure the following Goal: Pastor John plans to increase his membership by 1,000 people within the next 12 months. He currently has a membership of 500 members. He preaches 3 sermons per Sunday. Explain how he will reach his goal through measurable metrics:

1. How many members need to join per month?
   _____
   _____

2. How can he reach that many people? Name 4 ways He can reach that many people.
   _____
   _____

3. How many people will join because of these 4 efforts?
   _____
   _____

4. How often does the church need to execute the 4 objectives?
   _____
   _____

5. How many of the current members must participate to accomplish this goal?
   _____
   _____

Action-Oriented Goals:

Goals should not be idealistic and esoteric. A proper goal must have actions that can be taken. As believers, we often get locked in our prayer closets, when we should be working. James 2:14 informs us that "Faith without works is dead." Without action, your goal is nothing more than a wish, and God does not honor wishes. He only honors faith—living faith. Thus, if faith without works is dead (James 2:14), and "without faith, it is impossible to please God" (Hebrews 11:6), then by process of elimination, it stands to reason that without "action" it is impossible to please God.

Your faith should be seen in what you do. Your prayers should be heard through what you do. There's no need to be on your knees praying for hours. Your prayers are more powerful when you are on your feet working. Your work is your prayer. Your work is your faith. Each goal should be accompanied by action steps.

Think About It!

Create action steps for the following goal: Pastor John intends to build a community recreational center for the children in the community to enjoy, keeping them off of the streets. The recreational center will also provide other empowerment resources such as Tutoring, job training, GED studies and rehabilitation services. Name the 10 most important actions steps:

1. _____
2. _____
3. _____
4. _____
5. _____
6. _____
7. _____
8. _____
9. _____
10. _____

Realistic (or Reachable)

The worst thing a leader can do to his followers is set goals they cannot reach. The first rebuttal I expect to hear on this concept of reachable goals is that this statement lacks faith, because "I can do all things through Christ which strengtheneth me" (Philippians 4:13 KJV). Yes, we can do all things through Christ WHICH strengtheneth us, but not "all" things strengthen us.

God knows what we can and cannot handle. If I made a million dollars today, but was not mentally, emotionally, or socially equipped to handle that money, I would not be strengthened by the money, but weakened.

With that being said, leaders have to have an intimate understanding of their followers, and a compassionate cognizance of their strengths and weaknesses. God never dumps the entire vision on us because it is unrealistic and unreachable at our current strength. He takes us from "faith to faith," giving us small reachable goals that we can attain and grow from.

Your goal must be practical within the sphere of God. Within God's will, you can do greater than you could in your flesh. But if you've stepped out on your own to achieve the impractical, then you will fail. Set incremental goals. Set a 10% increase goal. To increase offering within the church, I helped my members to understand that we can't all give the "SAME" thing, but we can all give "SOMETHING". This strategy to challenge my members to increase their giving goals was successful. It created incremental, realistic growth, which lead to greater growth.

Think About It!

1. Do you know the strengths and weaknesses of your members/leaders? _____

2. Are you setting goals for them that they can actually attain through faith and their God-given gifts and skills, or are you pushing them to do the impossible?

3. Will your current goals strengthen your church or be a liability of time, energy, and resources?

Timetables:

Finally, there must be a set time. Goals without time are not goals; just ideas. Setting a time for your goal creates a sense of urgency and purpose. Achieving your goal "someday" is a worthless ambition. Someday may never come. Because humans are goal-seeking creatures, we are hardwired to respond with focus to a time-sensitive project.

The time-limit is set by the spiritual authority based upon need and resources available. Goals must be properly timed. A goal achieved out of order can actually be a detriment to the goal. As a leader, you must learn to have laser focus on details but also have a panoramic view of the big picture. Delegated leaders, however, are usually focused on their own timelines. Thus, the spiritual leader must coordinate the timetable.

When setting timetables, your expectations must be firm. The times set are not suggestions for your team, but they are important for the fulfillment of God's plan—if indeed we are fulfilling "God's plan." Leaders must instill the belief that our time is God's time. We should walk "circumspectly... redeeming the time" (Ephesians 5:16).

Follow-Up:

Lastly, after setting SMART goals, leaders must Follow-Up. Follow-up is a critical component to the success and execution of your goals. Goals are fluid and should be reassessed yearly, quarterly, monthly, week, daily and possibly hourly. It all depends on the goal and the time. As you execute your plan, you will come in contact with a number of unexpected challenges and variables that you did not expect. Your timeframe may be changed by weather; the company you hired may go bankrupt, your team members may quit.

Follow-up allows you to evaluate your objectives. It allows you to re-direct your efforts as you see fit, or restructure your team. A team member who was critical for Phase 1 of your plan, may be an obstacle in phase 2. An effective leader does not allow the goal to be put on auto-pilot, but mitigates step by step. During the follow-up, leaders reward those who are playing beneficial roles to the goal. These rewards go a long way in maintaining motivation amongst the team.

Effective Leadership: The Dynamics of Spiritual Authority

Think About It!

Example of a SMART Goal

Pastor John wants to raise $1,000,000 within a 12 month period to build the new community recreational center. He wants it built with little to no debt.

Time: 12 Months.

To raise $1,000,000 in 12 month, Pastor John has to raise just over $84,000 per month (rounding off).

Divide amongst resources.

Pastor John calculates 4 primary resources to meet his goal:

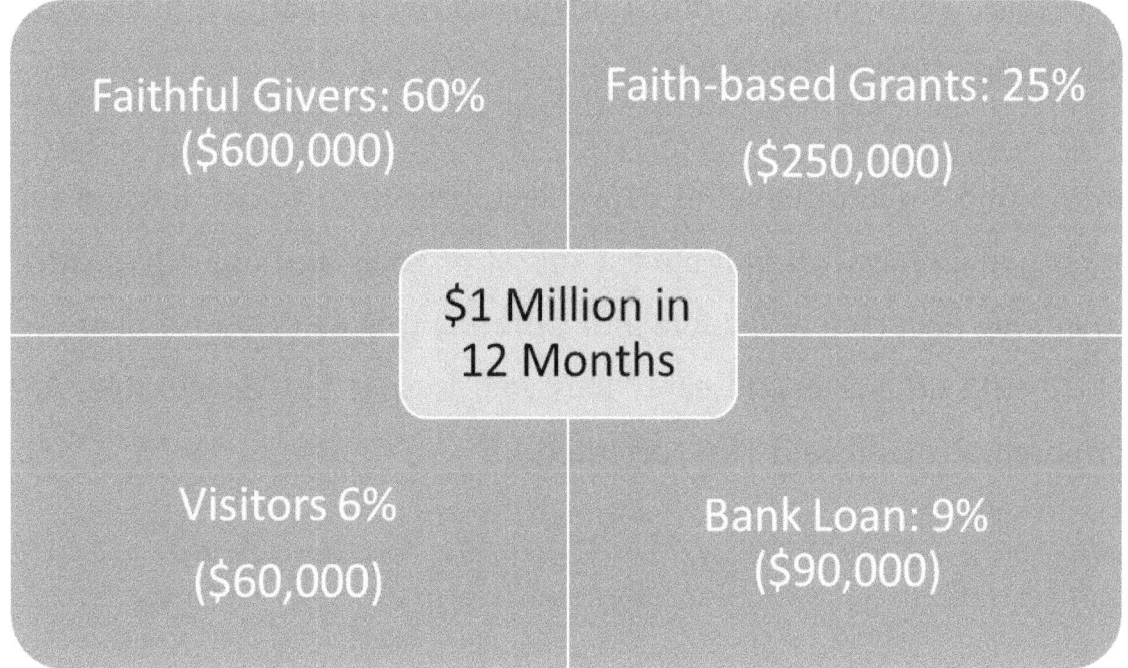

Faithful Givers:

Pastor John has 500 paying members. He plans to finance 60% of the goal through consistent church givers. By asking each member to give only $100 extra per month, Pastor John will raise $50,000 per month toward the goal and $600,000 within 12 months.

Faith-based Grants: Pastor John is aggressively pursuing faith-based grants. He plans to obtain a $250,000 grant for the community center.

Visitors: On a regular basis, Pastor John's church host 100 visitors per month raising and additional $2500 per month. Pastor John plans to start a campaign to increase visitors to 200 per month, increasing gifts to $5,000 per month. This will add $60,000 toward the goal.

Bank: Pastor John plans to utilize his great relationship with his local bank to finance the remaining $90,000.

Herein, we find a quantifiable, measurable approach to a goal. Each of the aforementioned objectives will have a subset of goals and objectives. Broken up among department leaders and workers, this $1,000,000 plan can be tackled with efficiency and ease. This goal is Specific, Measurable, Action-oriented, Realistic and Time oriented.

Dynamics of Motivation

Motivation is a big part of any organization and its achievements. Motivation starts with a need. People have basic needs and satisfying those needs leads to action. The desire to serve God and the church starts with a calling. Throughout scripture we see patriarchs called. The desire to please God motivated them. No man was more perfect in His desire to serve and please God than Christ. Christ is the perfect biblical example. He did not say no to the Father, God.

If we want to motivate the people, we will follow the steps Jesus set before us. Jesus called followers by name to serve. Jesus built relationships and called His followers brothers and sisters. He went where they were to get to know them, to be intimate. Jesus took time to listen and acknowledge sincerity. He looked at what people could be and shared that vision of their potential. Jesus led by example and entrusted others to carry out tasks He did and was willing to do Himself. Jesus never sought praise, many times telling the forgiven not to say a word.

As a leader, you must understand Christ has call you by name. See yourself as Christ sees you and His vision for you. If you are called to lead, embrace the authority given to you and be a shepherd to His people.

Understanding and utilizing Christ's examples, a leader can inspire others by also being a good example. Motivate by building relationships with each individual. Know their personal situations and call them to serve, always giving them the choice. See the potential in people and encourage them with the Vision of the church and how they fit in that Vision. Lead by example and be willing to listen, do, and teach while sharing that Vision. Do not seek praise but give it generously. Be specific with needs, plans, and desired outcomes.

The Bible is full of stories of prophets who were called. Many were asked to do things they did not feel they were particularly good at doing. Abraham was called to be the forefather of our faith with a wife unable to give birth. Jonah was asked to warn the people of Nineveh but he was not fond of them. Moses was said to have a speech impediment and was asked to be the voice of the Israelites. Peter spent the whole day fishing and did not catch a single fish. Jesus called him to be the Fisher of Men. A leader sees what his team can be, not what they are and motivates them to achieve greatness.

www.ingramcontent.com/pod-product-compliance
Lightning Source LLC
Chambersburg PA
CBHW081421080526
44589CB00016B/2622